James Payn

The Church of Jesus Christ of Latter-day Saints

It's Religion, History, Condition and Destiny

James Payn

The Church of Jesus Christ of Latter-day Saints
It's Religion, History, Condition and Destiny

ISBN/EAN: 9783337005078

Printed in Europe, USA, Canada, Australia, Japan

Cover: Foto ©Lupo / pixelio.de

More available books at **www.hansebooks.com**

THE CHURCH OF JESUS CHRIST
OF LATTER-DAY SAINTS.

Its Religion, History, Condition, and Destiny.

AN ADDRESS DELIVERED BEFORE THE ETHICAL SOCIETY,
AT SOUTH PLACE INSTITUTE, LONDON, BY

JAMES H. ANDERSON,

OF SALT LAKE CITY, UTAH.

A good tree cannot bring forth evil fruit, neither can a corrupt
tree bring forth good fruit.—MATT. vii, 18.

SALT LAKE CITY:
THE DESERET NEWS PUBLISHING COMPANY.
1892.

INDEX.

THE CHURCH OF JESUS CHRIST OF LATTER-DAY SAINTS.

OF THE religious denominations now in existence among men, none have attracted such attention from the others as the organization known as THE CHURCH OF JESUS CHRIST OF LATTER-DAY SAINTS, the members of which are popularly, though erroneously, called " Mormons," because of their belief in the divine authenticity of the Book of Mormon, a record of the ancient inhabitants of America. In every nation where the fame of this Church has spread, and where its Elders have appeared to teach their faith, one feature which stands pre-eminent is the bitterness with which they are opposed, without even the opportunity of being heard, principally by professed believers in Christianity.

Some there are who are practical in their adherence to the doctrine of religious toleration, and whose expansive minds lead them

to refrain from passing judgment till they
hear the case fairly stated. They hesitate
to follow popular clamor, preferring to ascer-
tain the truth for themselves, rather than
give assent to the voice of prejudice and
bigotry which demanded the life of Jesus of
Nazareth because He claimed to be the Son
of God. But these are the exception; the
rule has been to accept without question as-
sertions made against the Latter-day Saints,
and to decline to listen to anything in the
way of denial or justification. With this
prominent fact before us, it is beyond dispute
that to this organization above all others in
this generation must be applied the saying,
"For as concerning this sect, we know that
everywhere it is spoken against."

Doubtless much of this antagonism is due
to ignorance of the true belief, aims and condition of the Latter-day Saints. Certainly it
is largely because of gross misrepresentations
by those who have constituted themselves
their enemies. The reason for assuming this
position can be left for explanation to those
who occupy it. The purpose of the present
occasion is not to consider that branch of the
subject, but rather to present the doctrines
believed in by the Latter-day Saints, and the
reason for that belief. The limited time at our

disposal will admit of only a brief exposition of those doctrines; all who are desirous of more elaborate explanation may obtain it from the published works of the Church, and from its Elders, who will be pleased to present to investigators the Gospel message which they are proclaiming to the world The present opportunity is sufficient for but an abridged statement, in plain and simple language, of the religious system under consideration.

This Church presents no formula of religious dogmas. Its creed is: The direct revelation of God to His children. As He is without variableness, and is no respecter of persons, so His laws are unchangeable; and whatsoever He gives by the voice of revelation is a law unto the Saints. The organization of this Church was effected at Fayette, New York, on Sunday, the sixth day of April, 1830. Shortly after this event, its presiding Apostle and Prophet, Joseph Smith, was asked for a concise statement of what he and his people believed, and in reply he wrote the following:

ARTICLES OF FAITH OF THE CHURCH OF JESUS CHRIST OF LATTER-DAY SAINTS.

1. We believe in God, the Eternal Father, and in His Son, Jesus Christ, and in the Holy Ghost.

2. We believe that men will be punished for their own sins, and not for Adam's transgression.

3. We believe that through the atonement of Christ, all mankind may be saved, by obedience to the law and ordinances of the Gospel.

4. We believe that these ordinances are : First, Faith in the Lord Jesus Christ; second, Repentances, third, Baptism by immersion for the remission of sins ; fourth, Laying on of hands for the gift of the Holy Ghost.

5. We believe that a man must be called of God. by "prophecy, and by the laying on of hands," by those who are in authority, to preach the Gospel and administer in the ordinances thereof.

6. We believe in the same organization that existed in the primitive Church, viz: Apostles, Prophets, Pastors, Teachers, Evangelists, etc.

7. We believe in the gift of tongues, prophecy, revelation, visions, healing, interpretation of tongues, etc.

8. We believe the Bible to be the word of God, as far as it is translated correctly ; we also believe the Book of Mormon to be the word of God.

9. We believe all that God has revealed, all that He does now reveal, and we believe that He will yet reveal many great and important things pertaining to the Kingdom of God.

10. We believe in the literal gathering of Israel and in the restoration of the Ten Tribes. That Zion will be built upon this continent. That Christ will reign personally upon the earth, and that the earth will be renewed and receive its paradisic glory.

11. We claim the privilege of worshiping Almighty God according to the dictates of our conscience, and

allow all men the same privilege, let them worship
how, where or what they may.

12. We believe in being subject to kings, presidents,
rulers and magistrates, in obeying, honoring and sus-
taining the law.

13. We believe in being honest, true, chaste, benevo-
ent, virtuous, and in doing good to *all men;* indeed
we may say that we follow the admonition of Paul,
' We believe all things, we hope all things,'' we have
endured many things, and hope to be able to endure
all things. If there is anything virtuous, lovely or of
good report or praiseworthy, we seek after these things.

The position taken by the Prophet Joseph
Smith and those who have given heed to the
doctrines he presented is that they have no
new system of religion to offer to the world,
but that their message is the fulness of the
everlasting Gospel ; the Gospel which Paul
said was " the power of God unto salvation,
to every one that believeth ;" the Gospel of
which the Bible bears record, and which the
Lord Jesus Christ and His disciples taught as
the commandment of God to His children.
While they testify that it is a new revelation to them in this dispensation, " the
latter days," and that they received through
heavenly messengers sent from the throne of
the great Jehovah all the knowledge they
possess of the plan of salvation, and also the
authority to preach the Gospel and admin-

ister in its ordinances, they point out that it
is the same Gospel and divine message that
was revealed to man in ancient days ; the
"one faith" of which Paul spake to the Ephesians ; the Everlasting Gospel, *the* plan in-
stituted by God for the salvation of His
children—unchangeable, eternal, and trans-
cendently perfect.

Upon this presentation of the case, then,
are they to be judged.   They thus place
every principle or doctrine within the field
of comparison with the Holy Scriptures, both
in the Old and the New Testament.

THE GODHEAD.

The first of the Articles of Faith declares
a belief "in God the Eternal Father, and in
His Son Jesus Christ, and in the Holy
Ghost."   That is, that the Father is a per-
sonage of spirit, glory and power, possessing
all perfection and fulness ; the Son a person-
age of tabernacle also, who is the express
image of His Father, and possesses the same
fulness with the Father, in whose image also
man is created ; and the Holy Ghost, that
which bears record of the Father and the
Son, the life-giving element in all nature, the
agent of God's power, by which, through
faith, all things are controlled.   These three

constitute the Supreme governing power, the Godhead, and are one—above all, and in all, and through all—omnipotent, omniscient and omnipresent.

The idea thus set forth is that in form man is the image of his Creator. The Bible contains no suggestion of a similarity in form with any of the other creations of the Almighty. But with respect to man it is distinctly expressed in Genesis i : 26, 27 : "And God said, Let us make man in our own image, after our likeness, and let them have dominion over the fish of the sea, and over the fowl of the air, and over the cattle, and over all the earth, and over every creeping thing that creepeth upon the earth. So God created man in His own image ; in the image of God created He him ; male and female created He them."

Paul, in writing of God, says that Jesus was the "express image of His person" (Hebrews i : 3), being "in the form of God" (Phil. ii : 6). In the record which Matthew has made of the Lord's baptism, he describes the action of the three who constitute the Godhead : Jesus receiving the baptism of water, the "Spirit of God descending like a dove and lighting upon, Him," and a voice —the voice of the Father—uttering from heaven, "This is my beloved Son, in whom I am well pleased" (Matt. iii: 16, 17). The Redeemer of the world Himself testifies of their individuality: "For as the Father hath life in Himself; so hath He given to the Son to have life in Himself; and hath given Him authority to execute judgment also, because He is the Son of man" (John v: 26, 27); "Ye have heard how I said unto you, I go away, and come again unto you. If ye loved me, ye would rejoice, because I said, I go unto the Father: for my Father is greater than I" (John xiv: 28); "Nevertheless, I tell you the truth; it is expedient for you that I go away: for if I go not away, the Comforter will not come unto you; but if I depart, I will send him unto you" (John xviii: 7); "But when the Comforter is come, whom I will send unto you from the Father, even the Spirit of Truth, which proceedeth from the Father, He shall testify of me" (John xv: 26).

In the solemn prayer offered up before His betrayal, the Divine Master besought His Father, in behalf of His disciples; "That they all may be one; as Thou, Father, art in me, and I in Thee, that they also may be one in us: that the world may believe that Thou hast sent me. And the glory

which Thou gavest me I have given them;
that they may be one, even as we are one."
(John xvii : 21, 22).   The unity of purpose
and action in all things constitutes the one-
ness.   This union Jesus sought to bring to
His Apostles, that, each having his distinct
personality, they might be one, "even as we
are one."

MEN JUDGED BY THEIR WORKS.

"We believe that men will be punished for
their own sins, and not for Adam's transgression."

By this transgression death came into the
world, that men might gain the experience of
a mortal probation.   But that man should be
held responsible for an act in which he had
no agency would evidently be an injustice.
Our Father, being a just God, must therefore
deal justly with His children.   What is the
doctrine of the Scriptures respecting the res-
ponsibility of men?   In Jeremiah xvii : 10, it
is announced :   "I the Lord search the heart,
I try the reins, even to give every man according to his ways, and according to the
fruit of his doings."   As the laws of truth
and justice are inflexible in their operation
and effect, judgment as certainly follows evil
as blessings result from good deeds.

The beloved Apostle, in recording his vision
of the judgment, tells us: "And I saw the
dead, small and great, stand before God; and
the books were opened: and another book
was opened, which is the book of life: and
the dead were judged out of those things
which were written in the books, according
to their works. And the sea gave up the
dead which were in it; and death and hell
delivered up the dead which were in them:
and they were judged every man according
to their works" (Rev. xx: 12, 13). Language
can be no plainer to inform mankind of the
evidence that will be adduced for or against
them at the judgment-seat of Christ. It will
be their deeds; and from the judgment they
will make no appeal, for they cannot but
realize its justice.

By the divine law, man is answerable for
his own sins. He is not compelled to bear
the wrongs of another in the reward which
he will receive at God's judgment. The transgression of Adam was not ours, and can have
no ill effects upon us; it rather becomes a
blessing by the mercy of Jehovah. The Latter-day Saints believe that, as by Adam death
came into the world, without our action, so is
life the free gift to all men, through the atonement of the Lord Jesus. This is the doctrine

of the Bible. Paul expresses it thus: "Wherefore, as by one man sin entered into the world, and death by sin ; and so death passed upon all men, for that all have sinned : therefore as by the offence of one judgment came upon all men to condemnation ; even so by the righteousness of one the free gift came upon all men unto justification of life" (Romans v : 12, 18). The Lord has permitted no doubt to remain respecting the sins for which men will be punished and the good for which they will be rewarded. His word is: "For the Son of man shall come in the glory of His Father with His angels ; and then He shall reward every man according to his works" (Matt. xvi : 27). The testimony which He gave to John the Divine on the Isle of Patmos was : "I will give every one of you according to your works" (Rev. ii: 23); "And behold, I come quickly ; and my reward is with me, to give every man according as his work shall be " (Rev. xxii : 12).

THE ATONEMENT.

"We believe that through the atonement of Christ all mankind may be saved, by obedience to the laws and ordinances of the Gospel."

By this atonement is brought the victory

over death ; the resurrection of the body to
life ; the raising of man to a position where
he is not subject to death.   But it goes far-
ther in the article of faith read.   It brings
salvation by obedience to the Gospel.   Salvation, then, is more than a redemption from
the fall.   The latter comes to man without
his agency, so far as the mere restoration
to life is concerned.   That is the doctrine
which the Apostles taught :   " For since
by man came death, by man came also the
resurrection of the dead.   For as in Adam all
die, even so in Christ shall all be made alive "
(1 Cor. xv : 21, 22).   Since the Savior brought
to pass the resurrection and the life, His
atonement has a universal application, and
" there shall be a resurrection of the dead,
both of the just and unjust" (Acts xxiv : 15).

Does the atonement do more ?   The Latter-
day Saints reply in the affirmative.   Matthew
(chap. i : 21) records that the angel declared
to Joseph, when foretelling the birth of the
infant Jesus, "For He shall save His people
from their sins."   The Apostle Peter says :
" Neither is there salvation in any other : for
there is none other name under heaven given
among men, whereby we must be saved "
(Acts iv : 12).   By obedience to the laws and
ordinances of the Gospel, salvation comes to

man ; it is that which is added to the children of men by the atoning blood of the Redeemer, when the requirements of His Gospel are complied with. Until this is done, there is no salvation from sin. The Apostle John makes this unequivocal declaration : "This then is the message which we have heard of Him, and declare unto you, that God is light, and in Him is no darkness at all. If we say that we have fellowship with Him, and walk in darkness, we lie, and do not the truth ; but if we walk in the light, as He is in the light, we have fellowship one with another. and the blood of Jesus Christ His Son cleanseth us from all sin" (1 John i : 5, 7). If we would be cleansed from all sin by the blood of Christ Jesus, the condition is that "we walk in the light as He is in the light." If this be not our course, the Apostle says "we lie, and do not the truth." To these teachings is placed the seal and testimony of the Divine Master Himself, in His sermon on the mount : "Not every one that saith unto me, Lord, Lord, shall enter into the kingdom of heaven ; but he that doeth the will of my Father which is in heaven" (Matt. vii : 21). "In vain do ye worship me," said He to those who followed the tradition of men instead of keeping "the commandment of God" (Mark vii : 7, 8).

THE GOSPEL ORDINANCES—FAITH.

"We believe that these ordinances are : First—Faith in the Lord Jesus Christ."

The principle of faith is the moving cause of all action in intelligent beings. Faith in the Lord is the fundamental principle leading to obedience to His will. It is the assurance which we have of unseen things. By its exercise we are alone able to approach the throne of grace. "Without faith it is impossible to please Him ; for he that cometh to God must believe that He is, and that He is a rewarder of them that diligently seek Him" (Heb. xi : 6). It is not a mere passive belief ; but being a principle of action and power, it inculcates works in harmony with itself. The Savior says : "Let not your heart be troubled ; ye believe in God, believe also in me. Verily, Verily, I say unto you, He that believeth on me, the works that I do shall he do also ; and greater works than these shall he do, because I go unto my Father" (John xiv : 1, 12).

It is the belief of the Latter-day Saints that the Gospel is the working law of Christ ; that faith in Him, to have life, must be accompanied by works in accord with the mental exercise of faith. As the Apostle James says : "But be ye doers of the word, and not hearers only, deceiving your own selves" (i : 22). This

Apostle writes, "For as the body without the spirit is dead, so faith without works is dead also;" and in the second chapter of his epistle (verses 14—24) he states: "What doth it profit, my brethren, though a man say he hath faith, and have not works? Can faith save him? If a brother or sister be naked, and destitute of daily food, and one of you say unto them, Depart in peace, be ye warmed and filled; notwithstanding ye give them not those things which are needful to the body; what doth it profit? Even so faith, if it hath not works, is dead, being alone. Yea, a man may say, Thou hast faith and I have works: shew me thy faith without thy works, and I will shew thee my faith by my works. Thou believest that there is one God; thou doest well: the devils also believe, and tremble. But wilt thou know, O vain man, that faith without works is dead? Was not Abraham our father justified by works, when he had offered Isaac his son upon the altar? Seest thou how faith wrought with his works, and by works was faith made perfect? And the scripture was fulfilled which saith, Abraham believed God, and it was imputed unto him for righteousness: and he was called the Friend of God. Ye see then how that by works a man is justified, and not by faith only."

2

The Lord said, "Thou shalt love the Lord thy God with all thy heart, and with all thy soul, and with all thy mind. This is the first and great commandment" (Matt. xxii : 37, 38). He also explains what it is to love God : " He that hath my commandments, and keepeth them, he it is that loveth me : and he that loveth me shall be loved of my Father, and I will love him, and will manifest myself to him " (John xiv 21). This is faith .. and love of God : keeping His commandments.

REPENTANCE.

"Second—Repentance."

To those who, on the day of Pentecost, believed on the Apostles' words, and had awakened within their hearts faith in the Lord Jesus, Peter gave the law of the Gospel : "Repent, and be baptized every one of you in the name of Jesus Christ for the remission of sins, and ye shall receive the gift of the Holy Ghost. For the promise is unto you, and to your children, and to all that are afar off, even as many as the Lord our God shall call" (Acts ii : 38, 39). This law was universal in its application. It was " to all that are afar off, even as many as the Lord our God shall call."

When John the Baptist came in the wilderness of Judea, as the messenger before the Lord, preaching "the beginning of the Gospel of Jesus Christ, the Son of God," he proclaimed, "Repent ye, for the kingdom of heaven is at hand" (Matt. iii : 2). Of those who presented themselves for baptism he required conformity to the doctrine which preceded it. If they had not repented, the ordinance of baptism was refused to them. When many of the Pharisees and Sadducees came, he called them a "generation of vipers," and demanded that they "bring forth therefore fruits meet for repentance" (Matt. iii : 7, 8). God "commandeth all men everywhere to repent"—to turn from evil and walk in righteousness, for therein only is salvation. The Lord says, "Except ye repent ye shall all likewise perish" (Luke xiii : 3).

BAPTISM.

"Third—Baptism by immersion for the remission of sins."

To the repentant believer this is the "baptism of repentance for the remission of sins" taught by John the Baptist (Mark i : 4). On the day of Pentecost, Peter pointed the way to salvation, "Repent, and be baptized every one of you in the name of Jesus Christ for the remission of sins" (Acts ii : 38).

When the jailor sought to be saved, Paul and Silas "spake unto him the word of the Lord," and he "was baptized, he and all his, straightway" (Acts xvi : 30—33).

So important is this ordinance for admission into the Church of God, that the Lord Jesus insisted on receiving it at the hands of John the Baptist, who was authorized to administer it. John had preached that there should come after him One who should baptize "with the Holy Ghost and with fire," and when Jesus presented Himself on Jordan's banks, the Prophet recognized that mightier One. He felt his own weakness in the presence of the Son of God, and said, " I have need to be baptized of Thee, and comest Thou to me ?" But Jesus knew the law of God. He knew that it was necessary for even the Son of Man to enter at the door, and obey the ordinance which His Father had appointed. Therefore He answered John, "Suffer it to be so now, for thus it becometh us to fulfil all righteousness" (Matt. iii : 15). Then the Savior of the world went down into the river Jordan, and was baptized of John. When He came out of the water, there was given that glorious manifestation of the approval by His Father of the act of submission to the divine law, "and lo, the heavens were opened unto Him, and He saw the Spirit of God descending like a dove, and lighting upon Him : and lo, a voice from heaven, saying, This is my beloved Son, in whom I am well pleased " (Matt. iii : 16, 17).

If it was necessary for the Son of God, the Redeemer of the world, to receive the ordinance of baptism at the hands of one having authority to administer it, that He might "fulfil all righteousness," wherein can sinful man hope to enter by any other way ? And when that act of obedience to law on the part of the Divine Master was signalized by the glorious descent upon Him of the Holy Ghost, and brought forth from the Eternal Father the solemn declaration that He was well pleased with the Son who had just passed through the baptism of water, who among men dare say that the ordinance is vain, and useless, and non-essential ; that it is not of paramount importance to those who would do the will of the Father ?

The Lord also declared that the baptism of John was "the counsel of God"—this ordinance that was "the baptism of repentance for the remission of sins." Said Jesus: "All the people that heard him, and the publicans, justified God, being baptized with the baptism of John ; but the Pharisees and lawyers re-

jected the counsel of God against themselves,
being not baptized of him" (Luke vii : 29, 30).
As the Lord went forth in His ministry,
preaching the Gospel of the kingdom, there
came to Him Nicodemus, a ruler of the Jews.
To him Jesus said: "Except a man be born
again, he cannot see the kingdom of God"
(John iii : 3). Nicodemus did not fully com-
prehend this saying, and made further in-
quiry, receiving a reply in language that none
need misunderstand: "Verily, verily, I say
unto thee, except a man be born of water and
of the Spirit, he cannot enter into the kingdom of God" (John iii : 5). Therefore, when
the Master commissioned His disciples and
sent them out, after they had been "endowed
with power from on high," the command which
they received and obeyed was: "Go ye, therefore, and teach all nations, baptizing them in
the name of the Father, and of the Son, and
of the Holy Ghost: teaching them to observe
all things whatsoever I have commanded you:
and, lo, I am with you alway, even unto the
end of the world" (Matt. xxviii : 19, 20).

In this labor of the ministry, to which they
had been called and ordained of the Lord, He
fulfilled His promise, and was with them:
"And they went forth and preached everywhere, the Lord working with them, and con-

firming the word with signs following " (Mark
xvi : 20). The Apostles taught : " Repent,
and be baptized every one of you in the name
of Jesus Christ for the remission of sins "
(Acts ii : 38) ; " Know ye not, that so many
of us as were baptized into Jesus Christ were
baptized into His death ? Therefore we are
buried with Him by baptism into death : that
like as Christ was raised up from the dead by
the glory of the Father, even so we also should
walk in newness of life. For if we have been
planted together in the likeness of His death,
we shall be also in the likeness of His resurrection " (Romans vi : 3—5) ; " Buried with
Him in baptism, wherein also ye are risen
with Him through the faith of the operation
of God, who hath raised Him from the dead "
(Col. ii : 12). Here, then, is the Gospel doctrine : Baptism by immersion for the remission of sins, performed by one having authority ; the birth, the burial, the planting in
the watery element, without which ordinance
the Lord has said that no man can enter the
kingdom of heaven.

BAPTISM FOR THE DEAD.

It may be suggested that there are millions
of the human family who have not had the
opportunity of receiving of the baptism of re-

pentance by one having divine authority—
millions who never even heard of the name of
Jesus Christ. The Latter-day Saints believe
that the Gospel provides for all; that there
is and can be no exception; that every one
who will may partake of the waters of life
freely; that God is no respecter of persons,
but judges men by their works. A plan of
salvation that is adapted to the few, that does
not open the door to every being within the
great brotherhood of man, is unworthy of the
Creator and God of the universe. The Gospel
of the Lord must be perfect, even as He is
perfect, and reach to all humanity.

The query is made, How did the thief who
died on the cross enter the kingdom of heaven;
there is no record of his baptism? Let the
Scriptures give the answer: "And he said
unto Jesus, Lord, remember me when Thou
comest into Thy kingdom. And Jesus said
unto him, Verily I say unto thee, to-day shalt
thou be with me in paradise" (Luke xxiii:
42, 43). The Lord did not say he could enter
His kingdom, for He told Nicodemus that to
do that it was necessary to be "born of the
water and of the Spirit;" but He promised
the penitent thief that on that day he should
be with Him in paradise. Is that not heaven?
Let us examine and see, for on the proper

ascertainment of this fact depends a great principle of truth.

The body of Jesus was three days in the tomb, when the spirit again entered into it. When the Redeemer had risen, Mary came to the sepulchre and found that the body of her Master was not there. She began to inquire, when she heard a voice which she recognized as that of the Lord, to whom she turned. "Jesus saith unto her, Touch me not, for I am not yet ascended to my Father : but go to my brethren, and say unto them, I ascend unto my Father, and your Father ; and to my God, and your God" (John xx : 17). Here is the testimony of Jesus Himself, that during the three days subsequent to His crucifixion, while His body lay in the tomb, His spirit did not go to heaven or the presence of His Father. Logically, it must follow, neither did that of the thief.

Where, then, did he go? As Jesus was not in His Father's presence during these three days, where was He? The Scriptures have not left us in doubt upon this point. Jesus transferred to Peter the keys of the kingdom of heaven, and placed him at the head of the Twelve Apostles. Surely he is a competent witness ; he says : "For Christ also hath once suffered for sins, the Just for the unjust, that

He might bring us to God, being put to death in the flesh, but quickened by the Spirit : by which also He went and preached unto the spirits in prison " (1 Peter iii : 18, 19). During the time of His absence from the body He was preaching "unto the spirits in prison" —the place where the thief also went.

This doctrine of preaching the Gospel to the dead was taught by the Lord to His Apostles, just previous to His crucifixion : "Verily, verily I say unto you, the hour is coming, and now is, when the dead shall hear the voice of the Son of God : and they that hear shall live. Marvel not at this : for the hour is coming, in the which all that are in the graves shall hear His voice ' (John v : 25, 28). On the same subject, the chief Apostle says : "For, for this cause was the Gospel preached also to them that are dead, that they might be judged according to men in the flesh, but live according to God in the spirit " (1 Peter iv : 6).

The dead are to be "judged according to men in the flesh ;" and, as the Lord has declared that "except a man be born of the water and of the Spirit" he cannot enter the kingdom, what shall the dead who hear the voice of the Son of God" do ? Is the Gospel plan imperfect in that it does not provide a

way for those who have had no opportunity
to receive that birth? God forbid. Such an
injustice cannot be. Paul, writing to the
Corinthians respecting the resurrection, says:
"Else what shall they do which are baptized
for the dead, if the dead rise not at all? Why
then are they baptized for the dead?" (1 Cor.
xv : 29). The answer is complete: The dead
may be officiated for by those who dwell in
the flesh.

This is the doctrine of salvation for the
dead, an important part of the glorious Gospel that is as broad as the universe, and from
everlasting to everlasting. By receiving the
baptism for the dead, those who have passed
into the spirit world have opened to them the
door of the kingdom of heaven. "But one
man cannot act in the place of another," is
the suggestion that comes. The objector has
surely forgotten, or has not contemplated the
great truth that the whole Gospel plan taught
in the Scriptures rests upon the vicarious
atonement of the Lord Jesus Christ.

THE HOLY GHOST.

' Fourth—Laying on of hands for the gift
of the Holy Ghost."

When the Apostle Peter preached to those
who sought salvation, he said: " Repent, and

be baptized every one of you in the name of Jesus Christ for the remission of sins, and ye shall receive the gift of the Holy Ghost. For the promise is unto you, and to your children, and to all that are afar off, even as many as the Lord our God shall call" (Acts ii : 38, 39). Here is the offer to all of this blessed boon, the gift of the Holy Ghost, after baptism for the remission of sins. It was to them, and their children, and to all that are afar off. There was no exclusiveness in this ; the Gospel was open to all. By conforming to its laws, men receive the benefits of their own obedience. It is the great natural order of cause and effect. Comp. with the conditions, the result must follow. The sincerely repentant believer, baptized in the proper manner, and by an authorized servant of God, is entitled to the gift of the Holy Ghost as a matter of right.

How is he to receive it ? Just as did the baptized believers under the ministry of the Apostles : "Now, when the Apostles which were at Jerusalem heard that Samaria had received the word of God, they sent unto them Peter and John : who, when they were come down, prayed for them, that they might receive the Holy Ghost : (for as yet he was fallen upon none of them : only they were baptized in the name of the Lord Jesus.) Then laid they their hands on them, and they received the Holy Ghost" (Acts viii: 14—17); "through laying on of the Apostles' hands the Holy Ghost was given" (v. 18.) The Ephesians also "were baptized in the name of the Lord Jesus. And when Paul had laid his hands upon them, the Holy Ghost came on them; and they spake with tongues and prophesied" (Acts xix: 5, 6).

Of the office of the Holy Ghost the Lord says: "Howbeit when he, the Spirit of Truth, is come, he will guide you into all truth: for he shall not speak of himself; but whatsoever he shall hear, that shall he speak: and he will show you things to come. He shall glorify me: for he shall receive of mine, and shall shew it unto you" (John xvi: 13, 14). Here is the promise of guidance and revelation by the Holy Ghost. Its gifts are wisdom, knowledge, faith, healing, working of miracles, discernment of spirits, divers kinds of tongues, etc. (1 Cor. xii: 4—11). Wherever the Holy Ghost is bestowed, there are its gifts and graces manifest.

DIVINE AUTHORITY.

"We believe that a man must be called of God, by 'prophecy, and by the laying on of hands, by those who are in authority, to preach the Gospel and administer in the ordinances thereof."

The testimony of Scripture upon this is that Jesus "ordained twelve, that they should be with Him, and that He might send them forth to preach, and to have power to heal sicknesses, and to cast out devils" (Mark iii: 14, 15). To His Apostles He said: "Ye have not chosen me, but I have chosen you, and ordained you, that ye should go and bring forth fruit, and that your fruit should remain : that whatsoever you shall ask of the Father in my name, He may give it you" (John xv: 16); and of them, in praying to His Father, He testified: "As Thou has sent me into the world, even so have I also sent them into the world" (John xvii : 18). His Father had sent Him and had "given Him authority," and in like manner He gave authority to His Apostles. They in turn commissioned others to act in the ministry— "they ordained them Elders in every church" (Acts xiv: 23). As Paul has said, "No man taketh this honor unto himself, but he that is called of God, as was Aaron" (Heb. v : 4). Aaron was called by the voice of God, through Moses (Exodus iv · 14, 15).

The acts of those who are authorized to

officiate in the ordinances of the Gospel—to whom are committed the keys of the kingdom—are recognized by the Lord, and are given full force. "Whatsoever thou shalt bind on earth shall be bound in heaven ; and whatsoever thou shalt loose on earth shall be loosed in heaven" (Matt. xvi : 19). But those not authorized receive no such recognition.

OFFICERS.

" We believe in the same organization that existed in the primitive Church, viz. : Apostles, Prophets, Pastors, Teachers, Evangelists, etc."

The Apostle Paul taught that there was "one Lord, one faith, one baptism," and said of the Redeemer, "Wherefore He saith, when He ascended up on high, He led captivity captive, and gave gifts unto men. And He gave some, Apostles; and some, Prophets; and some, Evangelists ; and some, Pastors and Teachers" (Eph. iv : 8, 11). He also preached: "Now ye are the body of Christ, and members in particular. And God hath set some in the Church, first Apostles, secondarily Prophets, thirdly teachers, after that miracles, then gifts of healings, helps, governments, diversities of tongues" (1 Cor. xii : 27, 28).

God set these in the Church, is the

Apostle's testimony. Shall man say that they are not proper? The Lord has never changed the organization; on the contrary, these officers were given "for the perfecting of the Saints, for the work of the ministry, for the edifying of the body of Christ: till we all come in the unity of the faith, and of the knowledge of the Son of God, unto a perfect man, unto the measure of the stature of the fulness of Christ; that we henceforth be no more children, tossed to and fro, and carried about with every wind of doctrine, by the sleight of men, and cunning craftiness, whereby they lie in wait to deceive" (Eph. iv: 12—14).

Is there work for the ministry? Are the Saints yet to be perfected? Are we still far from the unity of the faith? Are we less than the stature of the fulness of Christ in the knowledge of God? With the present spectacle of jarring sects, religious discords, and disputations of doctrines, no intelligent person would venture to give other than an affirmative reply to these inquiries. There is evidently abundant work for the ministry, and therefore a necessity for Apostles, Prophets, and all the officers that God has set in His Church. Wherever that Church is organized upon the earth, there will these officers be found, with all the authority, gifts and powers that accompany the offices. The church which has them not is not the Church of Christ, according to the evidence presented by the word of God.

SPIRITUAL GIFTS.

"We believe in the gift of tongues, prophecy, revelation, visions, healing, interpretation of tongues, etc."

These are the gifts of the Spirit, which Christ promised should follow the believers. They are the signs which confirmed the preaching of the Gospel by the Apostles: "And He said unto them, Go ye into all the world, and preach the Gospel to every creature. He that believeth and is baptized shall be saved; but he that believeth not shall be damned. And these signs shall follow them that believe : In my name shall they cast out devils ; they shall speak with new tongues ; they shall take up serpents; and if they drink any deadly thing, it shall not hurt them , they shall lay hands on the sick, and they shall recover. So then after the Lord had spoken unto them, He was received up into heaven, and sat on the right hand of God. And they went forth and preached everywhere, the Lord working with

3

them, and confirming the word with signs
following" (Mark xvi: 15—20).

Of these are the miracles wrought by our
Lord and Savior. God hath set in the Church
"miracles, gifts of healings, helps, governments, diversities of tongues" (1 Cor. xii:
26). Never at any time has He said they
should be done away. He is an unchangeable being, a God of miracles to-day as much
as at any period of the world's history. He
cannot be otherwise and still occupy His
exalted position. He cannot be shorn of His
power to manifest the gifts of His Spirit
among the children of men, when the latter
comply with His laws. His arm is not
shortened, or His power to save diminished.
If miracles, and healings, and prophecy, and
the other gifts of the Spirit do not exist
among men, it is for the same reason that in
ancient days the Lord Jesus, in "His own
country," "could do no mighty work, save that
He laid His hands on a few sick folk, and
healed them," namely, "because of their unbelief" (Mark vi: 6, 7).

Those who dwell on the earth to-day are
equally the children of our Father with those
who lived nineteen centuries ago, and have
an equal claim on His blessings if they observe His laws and exercise the same faith in

Him as did His disciples anciently. "For
the promise is unto you, and to your children,
and to all that are afar off," said Peter, in his
proclamation of the Gospel, of which Paul
said, "But though we, or an angel from
heaven, preach any other Gospel unto you
than that which we have preached unto you,
let him be accursed " (Gal. i: 8).

THE APOSTASY.

The Latter-day Saints believe that but for
the apostasy of the primitive Christian
Church, it would have remained with the
same organization, powers and ordinances ;
with Apostles, Prophets, healings, miracles,
and all the gifts of the Spirit, up to the
present time. That these ceased to exist
among men is proof that there has been a
departure from the Gospel. If the organization had remained it would have been in the
same form as God placed it, and the true suc-
cessors to the Apostles would have followed
their example when they filled the vacancy
made in the Twelve by Judas's apostasy—by
selecting Matthias to be numbered with the
Apostles (Acts 1: 26). But there was no suc-
cession to the Twelve through the genera-
tions which succeeded them, therefore the
organization ceased to exist among men.

If there was to be an event of such importance in the world's history as a great apostasy, surely the disciples would have had an intimation of it through the inspiration of the Holy Ghost. By reference to their writings we find that they had this knowledge, and prophesied concerning it. Paul wrote to Timothy that the time would come when men would not endure sound doctrine, but would heap to themselves teachers, and turn away from the truth. (2 Tim. iv: 3, 4). He also taught that in the last days perilous times should come, when men should be "lovers of pleasure more than lovers of God; having a form of godliness, but denying the power thereof" (2 Tim. iii: 1—5).

To the Thessalonians was borne this testimony respecting the great apostasy: "Now we beseech you, brethren, by the coming of our Lord Jesus Christ, and by our gathering together unto Him, that ye be not soon shaken in mind, or be troubled, neither by spirit, nor by word, nor by letter as from us, as that the day of Christ is at hand. Let no man deceive you by any means: for that day shall not come, except there come a falling away first, and that man of sin be revealed, the son of perdition; who opposeth and exalteth himself above all that is called God, or that is wor-

shipped ; so that he as God sitteth in the
temple of God, shewing himself that he is
God. Remember ye not, that, when I was
yet with you, I told you these things ? And
now ye know what withholdeth that he
might be revealed in his time. For the mystery of iniquity doth already work : only he
who now letteth will let, until he be taken
out of the way" (2 Thess. ii : 1—7). The "mystery of iniquity" was making its influence
felt at that early day. Paul had warned the
people of what was coming ; as he says,
" When I was yet with you I told you these
things."

In the record of the vision given to the
Apostle John, which he says was " the revelation of Jesus Christ," we are informed that
John was shown " things which shall be here-
after." Of one of the beasts which he saw as
typical of a power which should rise up in
the earth, it is said, " And it was given to him
to make war with the Saints, and to overcome
them: and power was given him over all
kindreds, and tongues, and nations " (Rev.
xiii : 7).

This is some of the scriptural evidence concerning the great power which was to deceive
the nations of the earth and pervert the
Gospel by teaching men and women that

Apostles and Prophets were not necessary, and that the gifts of the Holy Ghost were done away, till Christendom has been brought to the apostate condition in which it is to-day. So complete was the work of this "mystery of iniquity," of the beast that "made war with the Saints and overcame them," that it was necessary for an angel to be sent from heaven with the Gospel message for mankind. John says of this event : " And I saw another angel fly in the midst of heaven, having the everlasting Gospel to preach unto them that dwell on the earth, and to every nation, and kindred, and tongue, and people" (Rev. xiv: 6).

THE BOOK OF MORMON.

"We believe the Bible to be the word of God, as far as it is translated correctly ; we also believe the Book of Mormon to be the word of God."

For people who believe the Bible to be the word of God to also believe that another record is His word, the two must be consistent with each other. There can be no conflict between them. For both to be the word of God, they must be divinely inspired, and their teachings be in perfect harmony. While it would by no means be certain that a record which has passed through so many hands as have the Bible manuscripts, with a loss of some, at least, of the sacred writings, would contain a reference to another record which was to be made by a separate branch of the House of Israel, yet it would not be unreasonable to hope that possibly an allusion to it might be found in some of the prophetic writings

This hope is not without foundation with respect to the Book of Mormon, which is a history of a part of the House of Israel, on the American continent. The Prophet Ezekiel says: "The word of the Lord came again unto me, saying, Moreover, thou son of man, take thee one stick, and write upon it, For Judah, and for the children of Israel his companions: then take another stick, and write upon it, For Joseph, the stick of Ephraim, and for all the House of Israel his companions: and join them one to another into one stick: and they shall become one in thine hand. And when the children of thy people shall speak unto thee, saying, Wilt thou not show unto us what thou meanest by these? Say unto them, Thus saith the Lord God: Behold, I will take the stick of Joseph, which is in the hand of Ephraim, and the tribes of Israel his fellows, and will put them with him, even with the stick of Judah, and they shall be one in mine hand" (Ezekiel xxxvii: 15—19).

The "stick of Judah" is the record which we have of the Jews—the Bible ; the "stick of Ephraim" is the other record, which we have in the Book of Mormon; and both records have become one in the hand of the Lord. Hosea says that to Ephraim had been written the great things of the law (Hosea xiii: 12), and the Savior informed His disciples of others that He must visit : "And other sheep I have, which are not of this fold : them also I must bring, and they shall hear my voice ; and there shall be one fold, and one shepherd " (John x: 16) These other sheep were to hear His voice—to receive a personal visit from Him.

The history of the coming forth of the Book of Mormon is, briefly stated, that its existence and whereabouts were revealed to the Prophet Joseph Smith by an angel sent from heaven. This angel said his name was Moroni, and that in the year A.D. 420 he had buried the sacred record in the hill Cumorah, which is located in the northern part of the State of New York. After Joseph had received several visits and had been instructed by the heavenly messenger, the plates were entrusted to his care, with a Urim and Thummim for their translation. Each plate was six inches wide and eight inches long, and not quite as thick as common tin. They were filled with engravings in Egyptian characters, and bound together in a volume, as the leaves of a book, with three rings running through the whole. The volume was something near six inches in thickness, a part of it being sealed. The characters on the unsealed part were small and beautifully engraved. The whole book exhibited many marks of antiquity in its construction, and much skill in the art of engraving. The Urim and Thummim consisted of two transparent stones set in the rim of a bow fastened to a breastplate. The unsealed portion of the plates was translated, and the whole were again taken charge of by the angel. The part which had been translated was published early in 1830, as the Book of Mormon, according to the command of God. It is an abridgment made by the Prophet Mormon, father of Moroni, from the records of his forefathers. On the title-page is this statement:

Wherefore it is an abridgment of the record of the people of Nephi, and also of the Lamanites; written to the Lamanites who are a remnant of the house of Israel ; and also to Jew and Gentile : written by way of commandment, and also by the Spirit of prophecy and of revelation. Written and sealed up, and hid up unto the Lord, that they might not be destroyed; to come forth by the gift and power of God unto the interpretation thereof: sealed by the hand of Moroni, and hid up unto the Lord, to come forth in due time by the way of Gentile; the interpretation thereof by the gift of God.

An abridgment taken from the Book of Ether also; which is a record of the people of Jared; who were scattered at the time the Lord confounded the language of the people when they were building a tower to get to heaven; which is to shew unto the remnant of the House of Israel what great things the Lord hath done for their fathers; and that they may know the covenants of the Lord, that they are not cast off forever; and also to the convincing of the Jew and Gentile that JESUS is the CHRIST, the ETERNAL GOD, manifesting Himself unto all nations. And now if there are faults, they are the mistakes of men: wherefore condemn not the things of God, that ye may be found spotless at the judgment-seat of Christ.

Several persons were permitted to view the plates, among the number being the "Three Witnesses," who thus testify of what they saw and heard:

THE TESTIMONY OF THREE WITNESSES.—Be it known unto all nations, kindreds, tongues, and people unto whom this work shall come, that we, through the grace of God the Father, and our Lord Jesus Christ, have seen the plates which contain this record, which is a record of the people of Nephi, and also of the

Lamanites, their brethren, and also of the people of Jared, who came from the tower of which hath been spoken ; and we also know that they have been translated by the gift and power of God, for His voice hath declared it unto us ; wherefore we know of a surety that the work is true.   And we also testify that we have seen the engravings which are upon the plates; and they have been shewn unto us by the power of God, and not of man.   And we declare with words of soberness, that an angel of God came down from heaven, and he brought and laid before our eyes, that we beheld and saw the plates, and the engravings thereon ; and we know that it is by the grace of God the Father, and our Lord Jesus Christ, that we beheld and bear record that these things are true ; and it is marvellous in our eyes, nevertheless the voice of the Lord commanded us that we should bear record of it ; wherefore, to be obedient unto the commandments of God, we bear testimony of these things.   And we know that if we are faithful in Christ, we shall rid our garments of the blood of all men, and be found spotless before the judgment-seat of Christ, and shall dwell with Him eternally in the heavens.   And the honor be to the Father, and to the Son, and to the Holy Ghost, which is one God.   Amen.   OLIVER COWDERY,
DAVID WHITMER,
MARTIN HARRIS.

From that testimony they never varied. They were separated from the Latter-day Saints, having departed from the Church, to which they belonged for a time after its organization.   But nothing could induce them

to change their statement. It was true, and
they knew it. In their old age Oliver Cowdery and Martin Harris returned to the
Church. David Whitmer never did. He was
the last to survive, his death having occurred
in January, 1888, at Richmond, Missouri.
When on his deathbed he called his family
and friends around him, and made to them a
solemn declaration that he knew the Book of
Mormon, and his testimony thereto, to be true.
Eight others also testify as follows :

THE TESTIMONY OF EIGHT WITNESSES.—Be it known
unto all nations, kindreds, tongues, and people unto
whom this work shall come, that Joseph Smith, Jun.,
the translator of this work, has shewn unto us the
plates of which hath been spoken, which have the
appearance of gold ; and as many of the leaves as the
said Smith has translated, we did handle with our
hands ; and we also saw the engravings thereon, all of
which has the appearance of ancient work, and of
curious workmanship. And this we bear record with
words of soberness, that the said Smith has shewn unto
us, for we have seen and hefted, and know of a surety
that the said Smith has got the plates of which we
have spoken. And we give our names unto the world,
to witness unto the world that which we have seen,
and we lie not, God bearing witness of it.

CHRISTIAN WHITMER,   HIRAM PAGE,
JACOB WHITMER,   JOSEPH SMITH, Sen.
PETER WHITMER, Jun.   HYRUM SMITH,
JOHN WHITMER,   SAMUEL H. SMITH.

Like the three, they never faltered in maintaining that what they had subscribed to respecting the Book of Mormon was the truth, and was with them an absolute knowledge.

Of further evidence concerning the authenticity of the Book of Mormon, there is in this sketch an opportunity of saying but little. Regarding the external proof, it must suffice to merely call attention to the developments of archæological research on the American continent. When the Book of Mormon was first published it was the accepted theory of the civilized world that America was not peopled by any nation of ancient times which had made marked progress in civilization But subsequently, from the appearance of Captain Dupaix's book in 1834-5, followed by the evidence of Lord Kingsborough, Stevens and Catherwood, Powell, and other well-known archæologists and explorers, a change came with respect to this matter, until now there is no doubt of the advanced position reached by ancient American civilization, as well as of the great antiquity of the native American races. The ruined temples and crumbling palaces of the ancient cities of Uxmal, Copan, Palenque, Quiché, and scores of others, whose architecture rivals that of any contemporaneous cities of the Old World, bear silent but incontrovertible testimony to the historical truth of the Book of Mormon.

With internal evidence of its divine authenticity, the volume is amply provided. It presents a code of ethics whose purity and godliness are unexcelled by any publication that has seen the light of day. In its pages there are no anachronisms and no contradictions. The various writers are in perfect accord. Compared with the great truths of science and nature, there are no absurdities and no inconsistencies. Between it and the Bible there is complete harmony in doctrine and in prophecy. It is a book that would be profitable reading to any thoughtful person. No intelligent, honest and sincere seeker after truth can give it thorough examination and consideration, with an understanding of the circumstances under which it was brought forth, without being convinced that in giving to the world the Book of Mormon, God has wrought one of the greatest miracles of any age or time.

REVELATION.

"We believe all that God has revealed, all that He does now reveal, and that He will yet reveal many great and important things pertaining to the kingdom of God."

When the Lord promised His disciples the Holy Ghost, He informed them that it would teach them all things (John xiv: 20); "He shall receive of mine, and shall show it unto you" (John xvi: 14). This was a direct promise of revelation through the medium of the Holy Ghost; therefore belief in revelation is a scriptural doctrine. It is the communication to men of knowledge from God: "Howbeit, when He, the Spirit of Truth, is come, He will guide you into all truth: for He shall not speak of Himself; but whatsoever He shall hear, that shall He speak; and He will show you things to come" (John xvi: 13). This is the word of the Lord—that the Holy Ghost should reveal things to come. The same condition which caused the withdrawal of the other gifts of the Spirit also caused the withdrawal of the gift of revelation. It was because of the apostasy—the unbelief of man. Never has the Lord said that He would reveal no more to the children of men. But He has forbidden men to add to or take from that which He reveals (Rev. xxii: 18, 19). When ever the Almighty has authorized servants upon the earth, there is with them the gift of revelation. "Surely the Lord God will do nothing, but He revealeth His secret unto His servants the Prophets" (Amos iii: 7).

The Apostle says that if a man lacks wisdom, and asks in faith for God to bestow it on him, He will do so liberally (James i: 6).

RESTORATION OF THE GOSPEL.

The tidings which the Latter-day Saints bear to the world are, that the Gospel has been restored to earth in this dispensation; that the present is the time of which Paul wrote, "that in the dispensation of the fulness of times He might gather together in one all things in Christ, both which are in heaven and which are on earth; even in Him" (Eph. i: 10). It is this restoration which John the Revelator saw in vision on the Isle of Patmos, and of which he says: "And I saw another angel fly in the midst of heaven, having the everlasting Gospel to preach unto them that dwell on the earth, and to every nation, and kindred, and tongue, and people, saying with a loud voice, Fear God and give glory to Him; for the hour of His judgment is come: and worship Him that made heaven, and earth, and the sea, and the fountains of waters" (Rev. xiv: 6, 7).

The Latter-day Saints testify that this angel has appeared, and has restored the Gospel, which is now being preached to the nations. It is the same now as anciently, with all the gifts, powers and blessings. Nothing is lacking. It is presented to all people for their consideration. The most thorough investigation is invited. There is nothing to conceal or hold back. It is not the province of the Gospel to put its light under a bushel, but to entreat all men to come forward and test its truth. "Prove all things; hold fast that which is good," was the admonition of the Apostle Paul; the same invitation is extended to-day.

Men are given intelligence; they are in possession of reasoning power. It is an insult to Deity to say that He forbids us to use these in seeking for knowledge. He asks for intelligent conformity to the eternal laws of truth, not for blind obedience to the dogmas of men. He has given to man his free agency. As expressed in the hymn:

"Know this, that every soul is free
    To choose his life and what he'll be;
    For this eternal truth is given,
    That God will force no man to heaven.

"He'll call, persuade, direct aright—
    Bless him with wisdom, love and light—
    In nameless ways be good and kind,
    But never force the human mind.

4

" Freedom and reason make us men;
  Take these away, what are we then?
  Mere animals, and just as well
  The beasts may think of heaven or hell."

This free agency was recognized by the
Divine Master, who said to the Jews, "Search
the Scriptures ; for in them ye think ye have
eternal life: and they are they which testify
of me" (John v: 39). To this testimony and
counsel of the Lord the Latter-day Saints
direct attention.

OTHER DOCTRINES.

Of the other principles believed in by the
Latter-day Saints there is not upon this occasion opportunity to speak at length. These
are: The Gathering of Israel ; the Restoration of the Ten Tribes ; the Support of
Earthly Governments for the Protection of
Human Rights; the Building up of Zion
and Re-building of Jerusalem ; the Resurrection ; the Second Coming of Christ to
reign as Lord of lords and King of kings—
all of which are doctrines of the Bible, as
clearly maintained in its teachings as those
which have been spoken of.

It may be well to refer to their ordinance of
marriage, of which there appears to be such
a misunderstanding in the world. This can

be briefly stated. The Latter-day Saints believe that marriage is ordained of God; that He has revealed to them its everlasting covenant; that when the ceremony is performed by His authority, the union of husband and wife is eternal—that it is bound on earth and bound in the heavens. "And they twain shall be one flesh: so then they are no more twain, but one flesh. What therefore God hath joined together, let not man put asunder" (Mark x: 8, 9). It is a covenant that is entered into voluntarily by the parties; there can be no compulsion in this, or in any of the ordinances of the Gospel. The Saints also believe that the patriarchal order of marriage, which was observed by holy men and women of old, is in consonance with the laws of God and of nature. This order includes a plurality of wives, as it was taught and practiced by Prophets of God in ancient times. Many people revile against it, frequently because they are ignorant of its harmony with natural laws, but it ill becomes those who profess a belief in Christianity to say that God ever gave to His children a law that was sinful in its nature or pernicious in its effects; to thus reproach the justice and righteousness of the Almighty is blasphemy.

With the Latter-day Saints the principle of

celestial marriage is the union of husband and
wife for time and eternity. They believe the
family relation exists in the celestial kingdom of God. They also have pronounced
views upon the purpose of the union of the
sexes. They do not believe that its object is
the gratification of passion, but that such an
idea is wicked in its inception and damning in
its practice. They believe that a departure
from the paths of virtue is punishable by the
severest penalties, and that the violation of
the marriage covenant is an offense which
ranks next to the crime of murder.

A GLANCE AT HISTORY.

The Prophet Joseph Smith was born at
Sharon, Windsor County, Vermont, U.S.A.,
December 23, 1805, his father being a farmer.
In the spring of the year 1820, when Joseph
was a little over fourteen years of age, he became deeply interested in religious matters.
He read the passage in James i: 5: "If any
of you lack wisdom, let him ask of God, that
giveth to all men liberally, and upbraideth
not, and it shall be given him." With full re-
liance upon that promise in the Divine Word,
this humble lad prayed to God and received
the heavenly manifestation. He continued
faithful and was instructed by messengers

from heaven, and received and brought forth the Book of Mormon. When these facts became known to the people in the vicinity of where he resided, he was made the object of false and slanderous reports, and severe persecutions. Many attempts were made to kill him, and every device was used to get the plates from him ; but the Lord protected him, and people began to believe his testimony. In 1829, John the Baptist came and ordained him to the Aaronic Priesthood ; in the same year the Apostles Peter, James and John ordained him to the Apostleship.

In obedience to the command of God, the Church of Jesus Christ was once more organized on the earth, with the promise from the Lord that it would never again be taken from among men ; that it was restored preparatory to the ushering in of Christ's millennial reign on earth. Some of its members were ordained and sent out to preach. Those who received their testimony and were baptized were filled with the Holy Ghost by the laying on of hands, and the word was confirmed with signs following. The Church rapidly increased in membership, and branches were organized in many of the States. A Temple was erected in Kirtland, Ohio. The State of Missouri became

the principal place for the gathering of the
people; but because they would not join in
the practices of the lawless element there,
and were believers in an unpopular religion,
an organized mob drove them from their
habitations, contrary to law, justice and humanity, to wander on the bleak prairies, in
wintry weather, till they left the tracks of
their bleeding feet on the frozen ground.
Men, women and children were subjected to
the most fiendish outrages—starved, tortured,
butchered. This was in a land that boasted
of religious freedom and tolerance!

Finally, about twelve thousand who had
escaped the exterminating order of Missouri's
mob found a resting place in Illinois, and
built up the beautiful city of Nauvoo. But
the refuge was only temporary, for the bigot
and the criminal united in a relentless and
bloody warfare upon them. Less than six
years after their expulsion from Missouri,
their Prophet was assassinated in Carthage
jail, while in the hands of the officers of the
law, and under the pledged protection of the
governor of the State, Thomas Ford. This
was on June 27, 1844. Joseph Smith had
committed no offense; he was guilty of no
wrong. "The law cannot reach him, but
powder and ball shall!" was the cry of his

murderers. The blood of the martyred Prophet and his fellow-religionists still cries to God for vengeance!

The enemies of the Saints, however, were doomed to disappointment, for the death of the Prophet did not stop the work, or break up the Church organization. The leadership devolved on the Twelve Apostles, with Brigham Young as their President; even greater energy was displayed than before, and the Temple at Nauvoo was soon completed. Fiendish plots were laid, and barbarous plans adopted to blacken the character of the "Mormon" people, and make them appear abominable in the eyes of the public. Numerous atrocities were committed by the mobocrats, who falsely attributed them to the Saints, and thus aroused public indignation against them.

Hoping to secure immunity from these unjustifiable attacks, they consented to move from the State, the mob agreeing to allow them to remain in peace a given time, so the exodus could be accomplished. This agreement was soon disregarded by the persecutors, who were reckless, and impatient to despoil the Saints. When a portion of the latter had left Nauvoo, the remnant was attacked by an armed force, and driven into Iowa in a destitute condition. General Thomas L. Kane, of Philadelphia, who passed that way a few days afterward, related his experience in a lecture before the Historical Society of Pennsylvania. The following is an extract from his address : "Dreadful, indeed, was the suffering of these forsaken beings ; bowed and cramped by cold and sunburn, alternating as each weary day and night dragged on, they were, almost all of them, the crippled victims of disease. They were there because they had no homes, nor hospital, nor poor-house, nor friends to offer them any. They could not satisfy the feeble cravings of their sick ; they had not bread to quiet the fractious hunger-cries of their children. Mothers and babes, daughters and grandparents, all of them alike, were bivouacked in tatters, wanting even covering to comfort those whom the sick shivers of fever were searching to the marrow. These were Mormons, famishing in Lee County, Iowa, in the fourth week of the month of September, in the year of our Lord 1846. The city—it was Nauvoo, Illinois. The Mormons were the owners of that city, and the smiling country around. And those who had stopped their plows, who had silenced their hammers, their axes, their shuttles, and their workshop wheels; those who had put out their fires, who had eaten their food, spoiled their orchards, and trampled under foot their thousands of acres of unharvested bread—these were the keepers of their dwellings, the carousers in their Temple, whose drunken riot insulted the ears of their dying."   Bancroft Library

Out into the trackless American wilds, into an Indian country, the "Mormons" wended their way, weary and destitute, for more than fifteen hundred miles, their pathway being marked by the graves of their dead. The history of their privations and sufferings is harrowing in the extreme. The lives of not less than a thousand of their number were sacrificed in the relentless persecutions connected with the exodus from Illinois. But God opened their way, and as a result of their unity, humility and faith through severe tribulations and deep sorrows, they were guided to a refuge in the valley of the Great Salt Lake. Three years later, in 1850, Congress created the Territory of Utah. Under the territorial form of government, the governor, secretary, judges, marshals, postmasters, election and other territorial officers, are appointed by the President of the United States.   Bancroft Library

In their new home, the Saints increased in

numbers, and were beginning to enjoy some of the comforts of life as a reward of their toil, when, in 1857, the national government was induced, through the misrepresentations of some of its officials, to send an army against the "Mormons," who prepared for another exodus, and to defend themselves. But the time required in such an undertaking gave the government an opportunity to discover that it had been misled, and to change its course. The record of the expedition, with its expenditure of twenty millions of dollars, stands as a monument of the folly of judging a matter hastily.

The current of popular opinion, however, had set in strongly against the Saints, and it is difficult to change it; but the majority of those with whom they are now in contact are not the lawless element of Missouri and Illinois, so that the violence of former times is no longer used against the body of the people where they are known. But the adverse feeling has caused legislation hostile to them. One feature of their religion that has been attacked is plurality of wives. Now that they have contested the question legally to the highest court in the land, where the decision has been unfavorable to them, they bow to the law, content to leave the issue between the nation that has raised its hand against them, and the God of Israel, in whose justice, mercy and omnipotence they have perfect confidence. Their Church property has also been seized by the government—property which was the voluntary gift of Church members, for the support of the poor, the building of Temples to the Lord, and similar purposes.

PRESENT CONDITION.

The results of the industry, integrity and thrift of the Saints, as shown by their present condition, are a complete refutation of the accusations of evil made against them. A corrupt tree cannot bring forth good fruit. Utah, the chief centre of their gathering place, has a population of 210,000, seventy-five per cent. being "Mormons." Ninety per cent. of the heads of families live in their own houses and on their own lands. The fruitful orchards, rich fields and farms, successful industries, and beautiful cities, towns and villages, present to the view a paradise upon earth ; while the vigor and cheerfulness of old and middle-aged and young betoken the health, prosperity and happiness which are God's own gifts to this people, in whose hearts dwells more abundantly than in those of any other community that love of God and of their fellow men which is the fruit of a pure and noble life in the service of the great Creator.

Not alone in Utah do the Latter-day Saints find a home. Their hundreds of settlements bedeck the mountain valleys from the province of Alberta, in Canada, through Montana, Idaho, Nevada, Wyoming, Utah, Colorado, Arizona, and New Mexico, in the United States, to Chihuahua, in Old Mexico, on either side of a line which reaches fifteen hundred miles along the backbone of the American continent.

As an ecclesiastical organization, the first officers in the Church are divinely commissioned Apostles of the Lord Jesus, and divine authority is possessed by the whole body of Priesthood, down to the office of Deacon. Almost the entire male membership of the Church is included in this classification; while there are organizations for the women and children. About three hundred districts, or wards, are united in larger organizations called Stakes of Zion, all combining in a perfect system.

FUTURE DESTINY.

The Saints have an abiding faith in the

future glorious destiny of the work in which they are engaged. From its inception there has been steady and rapid progress. Its Elders have carried the glad tidings to the nations as God has given them strength. They have not preached for money nor divined for hire. Freely they have received ; freely they give. Persecution has followed those who have obeyed the Gospel, just as it did anciently. But with each wave of adversity the Church has grown stronger, and its opponents have been restricted in their ability to inflict injuries on its members. Each successive blow of its foes has fallen more lightly than the one which preceded it ; while the Saints have been brightened and made better by the experience gained in drawing nearer to the Lord. No Latter-day Saint has any doubt of the ultimate triumph of the principles he has received in the Gospel. They form the plan of life, the power of God unto salvation. The Church is organized never again to be overcome. Its destiny is to continue to increase until its Founder and Head, the Lord Jesus Christ, will establish His eternal kingdom, and righteousness shall rule from the rivers to the ends of the earth.

THE GOSPEL MESSAGE.

The purpose of the Gospel is to lead us back to God, improved by the knowledge and experience we have gained. There is no truth in any department of life that is without its pale ; no knowledge that is beyond its reach. Its truth is the sum of all existence, the knowledge of things that have been, that are, and that will be. God is truth, and His Gospel is the plan whereby we may be saved in His presence. This is the doctrine that our Lord and Savior taught; this is the message given to the Latter-day Saints, and which they proclaim to the world. They call upon all men to repent and do the will of God. They invite sincere seekers after truth everywhere. They present to the world an example of the marvelous power of the Gospel they have obeyed. By their fruits they show its effects. They have solved the problem of a happy, prosperous and contented life, free from sin and sorrow, from poverty and idleness, from hatred and hypocrisy. They present to the rest of mankind the example of a people who put into practice their belief in being honest, industrious, true, chaste, benevolent, and in doing good to all men. If there is anything virtuous, lovely, or of good report, or praiseworthy, they seek after those things.

To all men they bear the message of the Gospel which has made them thus. They leave no room for deceit and delusion. They claim to have divine authority and divine principles, and they offer the proof, which is in the reach of every true, honest, virtuous man and woman. It is the test which the Lord has commanded them to proffer to mankind, the same that He applied to Himself: "My doctrine is not mine, but His that sent me. If any man will do His will, he shall know of the doctrine, whether it be of God, or whether I speak of myself" (John vii: 16, 17).

There can be no mistake about it, for if it be not of God, He will not give the knowledge. But tens of thousands of Latter-day Saints bear witness that they have received the testimony from Him. It is true, and we bear you witness now of its truth. Hereby we know that we know Him, that we keep His commandments. The Apostle John says: "Whosoever transgresseth, and abideth not in the doctrine of Christ, hath not God. He that abideth in the doctrine of Christ, he hath both the Father and the Son. If there come any unto you, and bring not this doc-

trine, receive him not into your house, neither
bid him God speed: for he that biddeth him
God speed is partaker of his evil deeds"
(2 John: 9—11).

That we do bring this doctrine, and that it
is true, is the testimony which we now give,
and which we will meet before the pleasing
bar of the Great Jehovah, the eternal Judge
of both quick and dead. And may the grace
of God the Father, whose throne is high in
the heavens, and the Lord Jesus Christ, who
sitteth on the right hand of His power until
all things shall become subject unto Him, be
and abide forever with those who seek to
serve Him in spirit and in truth. Amen.